Num
Find Out Your

Descrierea CIP a Bibliotecii Naționale a României
Numerology made easy : find out your destiny and purpose in life. -
București : My Ebook, 2016
 ISBN 978-606-983-009-3

133.5:511

©Copyright My Ebook Publishing House, 2016

NUMEROLOGY MADE EASY
FIND OUT YOUR DESTINY AND PURPOSE IN LIFE

My Ebook Publishing House
Bucharest, 2016

TABLE OF CONTENTS

I. VALUES

II. CALCULATION

1. THE DESTINY
2. THE PURPOSE OF LIFE
3. THE CHARACTER OF THE RELATIONSHIP WITH ANOTHER PERSON
4. ESTABLISHING THE INFLUENCE OF A COUNTRY, LOCALITY, INSTITUTION, PROFESSION, ETCETERA
5. THE MEANING OF A CERTAIN DAY
6. THE KARMA OF THE YEAR
7. LUCKY NUMBERS
8. WILL-HANDINESS
9. KNOWLEDGE AND SCIENCES
10. MARRIAGE-ACTIVITY-ACTION
11. ACCOMPLISHMENT
12. RELIGION
13. THE TEMPTATION
14. VICTORY
15. CORRECTNESS-BALANCE

16. WISDOM-SMARTNESS
17. CHANGING LUCK
18. SPIRITUAL FORCE
19. SACRIFICE AND SUFFERANCE
20. TRANSFORMATION AND DEATH
21. REGENERATION THROUGH EDUCATION AND RESTRICTION
22. MAGIC AND FATALITY
23. ACCIDENT-CATASTROPHE
24. TRUTH-FAITH-HOPE
25. DECEPTION-FAKE FRIENDS
26. GOOD LUCK AND FRIENDS
27. AWAKENING-REBIRTH
28. TO OBTAIN SUCCESS
29. BREAKDOWN-WRONG ACTION-SELF-DECEPTION

I. VALUES

Numerology is a way to find out the destiny and the purpose of life

The values of the letters:

A=1
B=2
C=11
D=4
E=5
F=17
G=3
H=8
I, J=10
K=11
L=12
M=13
N=14
O=16
P=17
R=20
Q=19
S=21
T=9
U, V, W=6
X=15
Y=10

Z=7

II. CALCULATION

1. THE DESTINY

What is given to accomplish in this life. For exemplification, let us take the name Iliescu Ion.

a) It is calculated the sum of the numbers that correspond to each letter from the name of the person for whom is made the calculus:

I L I E S C U   I O N
10+12+10+5+21+11+6+10+16+14=75+40=115

b) From this amount is subtracted the sum of the letters that compose it: 115-(1+1+5)=108

c) This number will be divided by nine: 108:9=12

d) And now it is added one: 12+1=13

Thirteen represents the number of the destiny, which you can find out by reading at this number: 13=Transformation and death.

2. THE PURPOSE OF LIFE

What is good to follow in a conscious way to accomplish in life, the person for which the calculus is made.

a) It is calculated the sum of the digits that compose the date of birth, in our case 3.3.1930.

3+3+ (1+9+3+0) =19

b) It is calculated the sum of the digits calculated for the name: 115+19=134

c) Hereinafter are renewed the accounts according the model shown before:

134- (1+3+4) =126; 126:9=14; 14+1=15

This number shows the purpose of life: Magic and fatality.

3. THE CHARACTER OF THE RELATIONSHIP WITH ANOTHER PERSON

For example, Cimpeanu Radu.

a) At first is calculated the sum of the digits corresponding to each letter of the name Cimpeanu Radu like at the point 1.a). We obtained 108. Check!

b) Are added the corresponding sums: 115+108=223

c) Are renewed the accounts according to the model we learned: 223- (2+2+3)=216; 216:9=24; 24+1=25

d) In all cases in which, like here, the number obtained is greater than twenty two, are added the component digits of the number obtained: 2+5=7, Victory.

Comments: we consider natural this result, from the moment the opposition participates constructively at the political and economical life of a state, making "a couple" with the government forces. In a similar way it can be calculated the result of the association with a view of a common action of three, four or more persons.

4. ESTABLISHING THE INFLUENCE OF A COUNTRY, LOCALITY, INSTITUTION, PROFESSION, ETCETERA

a) Within our example, we calculated the number for Romania. We obtained seventy five.

b) This number is totaled with the one of the person's name and with the one of his birth date, being continued the calculus according to the example aforementioned: 75+115+19=209; 209- (2+0+9) = 198; 198:9=22; 22+1=23; 2+3=5, Religion.

5. THE MEANING OF A CERTAIN DAY

a) It is calculated the number of the day. For example 20.5.1990. (2+0)+5+ (1+9+9+0) =26.

b) This number is totaled with the one of the person's name and with the one of his birth date, continuing the calculus similarly with the known model. 26+115+19=160; 160-7=153; 153:9=17; 17+2=19, Luck and friends.

In the end is added two, not one!

6. THE KARMA OF THE YEAR

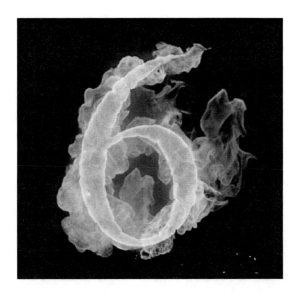

We took as example the year 1990. Are summed up the numbers of the year, of the name and of the date of birth: (1+9+9+0) +115+19=153
1553- (1+5+3)=144:9=16; 16+1=17. Truth, belief, hopes.

7. LUCKY NUMBERS

a) Determining the basic number: it is made by adding the numbers of the name (75) and the surname (40), resulted from summing the digits that compose them: 7+5=12; 4+0=4; 12+4=16

b) To this number is added and subtracted 9. 16+9=25; 16-9=7. The days of seven and twenty five of the month are lucky for him.

8. WILL-HANDINESS

The will, the energy, is an invisible force. The more wants the man, the more he deposits more energy, and the more accumulates more of this invisible substance.

The people with one must have for their projects a lot of trust, energy and fervor. And then they will be successful. The one that cannot do this, even though has the number one, will attract his breakdown and only he will be to blame for this.

The energy is the property to eliminate at once any disbelief. With this energy, with the force of the will of the spirit can be accomplished things that seem impossible. The persons with one have in any case the possibility to make to dominate the energy through an inner force.

The persons with one are very good engineers, technicians, inventors, but because ideas are coming toward them from all sides, most of the times they are scatterbrained. In this situation we will find the actors, scientists, diplomats, and so on.

9. KNOWLEDGE AND SCIENCES

The persons with two have a strongly developed intellect, being capable to receive all the knowledge of life and this is why they are teachers, professors, born writers. But they must be careful not to become fake scientists (because, being too vainglorious in their unverified knowledge, they can be wrong).

They are less creative, even though their preponderant activity is the one to assume the ideas of others, proving this way to be pioneers of science and culture, representatives and agitators. They build that category of persons which prove to be creative with the aid of others' knowledge. There is the danger to persist into a wrong opinion or to be limited in understanding and to not be able to overcome a certain limit.

They always search, as introducers of progress, to make the impression that they overcome their understanding capacity (they make affirmations that overcome their knowledge). They have too little originality (spiritual), so they always cling to intellect and matter (without taking into account the spiritual side). We find among them materialistic science men.

10. MARRIAGE-ACTIVITY-ACTION

The destiny of the persons with three is to get married, because only through a real marriage, therefore through their partner and children, they can evolve. It should be taken into account the fact that women are generally more subtle, and the men have a stronger intellect.

The woman makes public her intuition, and the man, with the aid of the intellect and logic, transforms this intuition in reality. The woman must not disturb him in choosing and following the path. The one that lives this way in marriage, live the true divine marriage. The wife transmits the spiritual force to the husband through sexual contact. She receives the seed from the husband, and transforms it, becoming able to inspire the husband.

These ways are the artists' muses, of the initiated. Through the transfer of the forces, the man also becomes more capable for his activities. The men with three, even though they get married, become more active.

11. ACCOMPLISHMENT

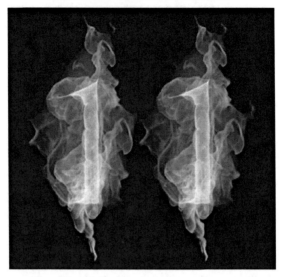

The men with the figure four have the mission to accomplish themselves. If they do not evolve enough, they will only succeed in a lower sense.

The evolved ones will acquire a correct understanding of the universe. But, for this evolution it is necessary a lot of perseverance which will manifest of course on the outside. These are the persons that one day will become aware that the road they took so far is wrong and that they could not progress because of all kinds of obstacles.

They must accomplish this inner work through themselves. The impulse toward this will always be caused by an exterior event. Then they will realize they walked on a wrong path; this acknowledgement is produced with a force that can crumble some. To avoid a wrong attitude in this sense, it is necessary an inner fight, which the humans with four posses for certain.

The force specific to them, through which they realize themselves must be guided on good paths. Contrariwise, these forces turn against them.

12. RELIGION

The persons with five are the humans which are aided by the spiritual force to go through all the blows of the destiny. They have an intense force of desire, and through it they will be successful. They must always believe in the omnipotence of God and to carry this faith within them.

There were always persons who, in the years it results the digit five, lose a loved one through separation or death. But the one that is aware that the death of a man is nothing but a passing (transformation) through which the one that leaves has been redeemed of his missions from this life, those must not despair or regret, but will tell himself that the death of a person does not represent anything tragic.

13. THE TEMPTATION

The persons with six will have in their destiny many temptations to which they must resist by any means. There are all kinds of temptations.

The mission of each person with six is the one to recognize them. The temptations are the bad thoughts that the man has, and they always strike in human also because, the way you shout in the woods, the same returns the echo.

Therefore, the one that has six must stay away from bad thoughts, because himself will be their victim.

14. VICTORY

Seven is a holy number and represents the human that can obtain the force of a wonderful action in life. In most of the cases, the ones with seven will obtain the victory over themselves, and through this, victory in all their existence.

They are humans with a healthy intellect, noble, turn up trumps in helping others: they get along well with their fellow creatures and wish them to have a good existence. They love the nature and reject generally all that is artificial.

They feel everything profoundly, socially, and wish to accomplish everything in life in association with others. It is not characteristic for them to act by themselves.

The ones with seven, found on a high step of evolution, will make great progresses in life and will act with competence in the most various directions. The back ones (or the negative types) will have certain successes in life, but in the end they will transform in disastrous breakdowns.

15. CORRECTNESS-BALANCE

Here especially is experienced strongly the law of balance in destiny. This law does not sanction just for the sake of sanctioning, but to bring the human at a superior happiness; any barrier, any malady, any material or psychic obstacle forms a sentence that has pronounced because of certain incorrect actions.

The purpose of life of the ones with eight must be healthy, a good spirit. The manifestation of the forces must be held in balance, because these people only this way will be good.

The one that associates with the divine justice, to that one the good happens all by itself. The persons with eight must act fair to remain in psychic balance.

16. WISDOM-SMARTNESS

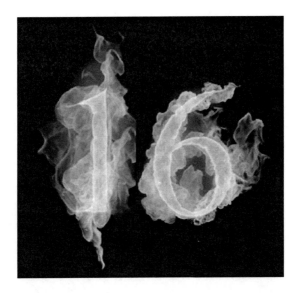

The people with nine are those beings that pick-up from the divine spirit the total wisdom. Because of this exceptional inclination, they are forced to transmit to others this spirit and do not have the right to keep it all for themselves.

If they transmit it to others, they will harvest a rich crop. Most of the times, the persons with nine act with wisdom and intelligent; or at least they have the necessary qualities for this. The people with a superior evolution will produce, because the force of their spirit, favorable transformations.

They will share selflessly the entire result if their spirit, to bring benefits to their fellow creatures. The people with nine are intuitive, original, selfless and dispose of powerful gifts of clairvoyance or perceptions, of which they are never allowed to use in selfish purposes.

17. CHANGING LUCK

The people with ten are subjected to a very changing destiny. In most of the cases, from the happiest situation they get unexpectedly in the opposite situation. It only depends to them to build the path toward luck.

The people with ten must try to live and act quietly, with calm. Because they tend to act fast, proving to be restless and agitated, they torch up fast but this fervor must never pass of the goal proposed. They must learn to master themselves. Even though the fervor is a gift that can have a magical effect, it can achieve high ideals.

They must have faith in themselves, tranquility, will and handiness-which they have to manifest in all actions. Then the success will be sure, because 10=1+0=1. Will, handiness.

18. SPIRITUAL FORCE

The spiritual force is the highest force the man has.

It makes these people carry a great responsibility for all their actions in such scale that they have to think very much before acting. The spiritual force gives capacities of clairvoyance and clearly perception that must never be used in unholy purposes.

The power to remain in a state of good disposition even in difficult situations of the destiny and to protect others in this kind of situations-this is the spiritual force. Only this way, these people will be successful in life. This psychic force that emanates from them will be received by other people, whom they will inspire courage. These people also have the capability to foretell certain things. They dispose of a sharp intellect, the gift to foresee and the self certainty.

The humans with eleven dispose also of the gift to heal through love and desire. They are perseverant in following their projects, but must not become scatterbrained; to always remain focused on the ideas they have to accomplish. 11=1+1=2. Knowledge and sciences.

19. SACRIFICE AND SUFFERANCE

The people with twelve have the mission to sacrifice for their family, for their fellow creatures, or for an idea. They are the people that love very much their fellow creatures and to which no sacrifice seem too big to not do it with pleasure.

They build that category of people that have mercy and feel the pains of others. They are withdrawn without emphasizing this isolation. 12=1+2=3 this means Marriage, activity, action. Marriage calls for a self sacrifice and here are applied these aptitudes.

Besides, the one that sacrifices for the family or for an idea will receive help from outside in the moment he will need it.

20. TRANSFORMATION AND DEATH

The transformation means change. The death of a human means a passing from the actual physical shell in the one purely spiritual and psychic in other spheres, in which the human prepares for the future reincarnation. Therefore any person with thirteen has the mission to transform from a more or less material human in a spiritual one.

This way he will accomplish his mission on earth, which he would have to accomplish ulterior anyway. Because of their leader peculiarities, the persons with thirteen are able to overcome all the obstacles, of any nature, easily. They must keep off from manifesting too much trust in themselves, because this will lead him to imprudent actions.

They also have the gift of foresight and of forecasting dreams. They must be careful with the dreams, because they will help him transforming. The one that does not realize this spiritual transformation will suffer a spiritual death and will be put in front of the same missions in the next life.

21. REGENERATION THROUGH EDUCATION AND RESTRICTION

The regeneration means renewing. The people with fourteen must renew because of their spiritual force. The one that did not progressed as fast as he imagined, not becoming pessimistic or fearful, not to be on the rack if everything goes on the opposite.

He must not hurry or rush, but must prove a lot of forbearance. If they cannot obtain anything because of some limits imposed by the destiny, they do not have to consume pointlessly the energy by proving pessimism or haste. The humans with fourteen must learn to wait because their time will come too.

They have to be temperate in everything, even in working, because it exists the danger to overstrain themselves. They do not have to try to do everything at once. They have to learn to save up to have for the rainy days.

22. MAGIC AND FATALITY

The people with fifteen dispose of powerful magical and magnetic capacities which they must use though only in good purposes, for helping.

They dispose consciously or unconsciously of the capacity to influence other people too, but these forces must be used only in selfless purposes. This way, his forces and actions will have a negative effect over themselves being what is called "dark magic".

The people with fifteen that use these forces to help the others do white magic and enjoy the good effects produced over them over the ones surrounding them. Who wants to obtain success through circumvention and elusions falls in the hand of the balancing force of the divine force.

The apparent successes obtained this way will be paid with twinges of conscience and physical and psychic illnesses. The ones that have fifteen and are aware of their magical forces will be tempted because 15=1+5=6, temptation.

23. ACCIDENT-CATASTROPHE

The people with sixteen, more than any others will suffer in their life many diseases, accidents, losses of money, catastrophes. They must stay away of doing hasty actions and untaught or bad actions, dodging excesses and exaggerations of any kind.

The one that has sixteen must not let himself mastered by fear, because through a spiritual and psychic evolution can make from 16=1+6=7, Victory. Therefore, through a correct life, he can obtain a victory over himself, and through this, over others as well.

There also exists the possibility for him to not be the one that is directly hit by accident and catastrophe, but indirectly, through the sufferance produced by the accident and the catastrophe over other persons that are close to him.

24. TRUTH-FAITH-HOPE

The person with seventeen (optimism), attracts success almost without contributing with nothing. Everything that is obtained in life, a pleasant body, a balanced psyche, a healthy spirit, pleasure, successes, everything depends only on them, on the force of good thoughts, optimistic.

Therefore, the ones with seventeen must always think honestly, clearly and with faith. Only this way the thoughts transform into reality, and the success will appear. 17=1+7=8, Correctness, balance.

The person with seventeen must act correctly to remain in a psychic balance.

25. DECEPTION-FAKE FRIENDS

The persons with eighteen are put to manipulations from the part of their friends, to be deceived. Therefore, they must choose their friends very carefully.

Because everything has two aspects, they must beware of being themselves deceitful or fake friends. Then they must beware of the bad society, because only this way they will avoid fake friendships.

The one that has eighteen must not establish relationships with painstaking persons, selfish, hot-tempered and suspicious, because they would become the same as them. 18=1+8=9, Wisdom, cleverness. Through wise action he can stay from deceptions and fake friends.

26. GOOD LUCK AND FRIENDS

The people with nineteen have in their life more good luck then others. They must always be careful to not ruin their destiny for the future life.

These people have the mission that the luck they live to transmit it also to their fellow creatures and not to hold everything in a selfish way for them. Only in this case they will have true friends. Even though nineteen means good friends, they can still be two types. Some, like always, settle in when the person is well.

Others remain even if he is straitened; in this case the friends from the first category draw back. The people with nineteen must analyze in their good period, of great luck, the character of their friends, to not be deceived later.

It must also be taken into account the fact that luck does not always come by itself, but only if he will prove a lot of will and competence, because 19=1+9=10, Changing luck.

27. AWAKENING-REBIRTH

The people with twenty live a renewal of their Ego until health, which will be fuller and fuller. A gradual renewal in the superior shape of their existence and a spiritual and psychic evolution, which few people achieve.

They will realize this only if they will have spiritual occupations, which will lead them to revelations that others cannot understand. Though, they have the mission to transform these revelations into reality and to live them, because, without action-the revelations are useless.

The rebirth consists into a total faith in God and in the divine wisdom. Intuition is the wisdom that manifests into us, because people with twenty are intuitive and skilled with clairvoyance and clear-perception.

28. TO OBTAIN SUCCESS

Generally, the people with twenty one achieve the goal they proposed. The higher the aim, the more they obtain.

Through activity, this kind of person will obtain a great success; but also for the life partner is possible to obtain material successes; these in return will serve him for achieving the goal proposed. Also, the partner can offer him the spiritual and psychic support, as well as the alliance in work.

The ones with twenty one will have in the second period of their life a happy marriage, the male or female partner being a person they match very well. But in successes he also has a great responsibility; to not become arrogant and always to act with a sense of responsibility toward their fellow creatures.

29. BREAKDOWN-WRONG ACTION-SELF-DECEPTION

Twenty two is the rarest number. The one that has this number must always be careful not to fall prey to illusions and to rationalize clearly over everything before acting.

Contrariwise, very easily he will act wrong, obtaining only breakdowns. Among these people we find the ones with unhealthy fantasy, fake prophets which seek to convince the others with their wrong prophecies.

Also, among these are found the ones that lie until themselves believe that lie. But through a clear spiritual attitude, these people can realize on a positive path, because 22=2+2=4, Accomplishment. The people with twenty two have almost exclusively material interests; rarely exists exceptions.

CPSIA information can be obtained
at www.ICGtesting.com
Printed in the USA
LVOW12s0308110417
530355LV00027B/575/P